EMPATH

----- ❧ ❦ ❧ -----

*A Beginner's Guide to Succeeding in Life
as a Highly Sensitive Individual*

NEAL D. ROSCHMANN

© **Copyright 2018 by NEAL D. ROSCHMANN - All rights reserved.**

The transmission, duplication or reproduction of any of the following works including specific information will be considered an illegal act irrespective of whether it is done electronically or in print. This extends to creating a secondary or tertiary copy of the work or a recorded copy and is only allowed with an explicit written consent from the Publisher. All additional rights reserved.

The information in the following pages is broadly considered to be a truthful and accurate account of facts and as such any inattention, use or misuse of the information in question by the reader will render any resulting actions solely under their purview. There are no scenarios in which the publisher or the original author of this work can be in any fashion deemed liable for any hardship or damages that may befall them after undertaking information described herein. The author does not take any responsibility for inaccuracies, omissions, or errors which may be found therein.

Additionally, the information in the following pages is intended only for informational purposes and should thus be thought of as universal. As befitting its nature, it is presented without assurance regarding its prolonged validity or interim quality. The author of this work is not responsible for any loss, damage, or inconvenience caused as a result of reliance on information as published on, or linked to, this book.

The author of this book has taken careful measures to share vital information about the subject. May its readers acquire the right knowledge, wisdom, inspiration, and succeed.

Table of Contents

Introduction 1

Chapter 1: Empath 101 3

Chapter 2: Advantages and Disadvantages of Being an Empath 17

Chapter 3: Being Happy as an Empath 35

Conclusion 57

Introduction

Congratulations and thank you for downloading this wonderful book!

The following chapters will teach you everything that you need to know about being an empath:

Chapter 1 talks about the basics so that you will have a good foundation and understanding of what being an empath really is.

Chapter 2 discusses the advantages and disadvantages of being an empath.

Chapter 3 teaches powerful meditation techniques and realizations that you need to help you live a happy life as a true empath.

There are plenty of books on this subject on the market. Thanks again for choosing this one! Every effort was made to ensure it is full of as much useful information as possible. Please enjoy it as much as you can!

Chapter 1: Empath 101

What is an Empath?

An empath refers to a person who has the ability to feel what another person is feeling. It includes the ability to place one's self in another person's situation or position. Some people are naturally born as empaths while others deliberately learn this ability. When you are an empath, then it means that you have the ability known as *empathy*.

People usually consider empathy as a gift, while others consider it as a curse. This is a matter of how you use it. This is why it is important to learn as much as you can about empathy so that you can use it in a constructive way. The more you understand it, the more that you can control it. Do not worry. By the time you finish reading this book, you will have the right knowledge that you need to understand what being an empath is all about. To begin with, let us look at the different theories about being an empath.

Theories

In spirituality, it is believed that man is more than a physical body. Beyond the physical body, there is what is called as the energy body. This energy body has different chakras. The chakra is as much a function of the body just as the physical body has its own organs. When it comes to being an empath, the chakra involved is the heart chakra. The heart chakra is located in the middle of the chest, and its color is yellow.

Now, let us look at what established science has to say about empaths:

- ***The Mirror Neuron System***

    Being sensitive to other people's feelings is an innate capability by most humans. This is because everyone has a certain group of brain cells, called mirror neurons, which specialize in being able to imitate the actions and feelings of others. Mirror neurons tend everyone to imitate strong emotions felt by another person. So, it is normal to also feel other people's happiness, fear, and pain. Like, for example, when you are in a hospital and everyone around you is worried. A feeling of worry will also creep over you.

Researchers say that empaths have hyper-responsive mirror neurons. They can deeply understand and share other people's feelings by having this type of mirror neurons.

In contrast, there are people who have under-active mirror neurons. These people cannot feel any empathy, unlike others. Such people like sociopaths, narcissists, and psychopaths are believed to have "empathy deficient disorders."

- ***Electromagnetic Fields***

Electromagnetic fields are generated by peoples' hearts and brains and empaths are very sensitive to these fields. This is because these fields can convey other people's feelings which empaths are highly tuned with. They sometimes feel them extremely and in turn, can sometimes overwhelm them.

Electromagnetic fields from the sun and earth can also significantly affect empaths. Their state of mind and energy are more influenced by the changes in these fields compared to a normal person's state of mind and energy. This is due to their deeper physical and emotional responses with the sun and earth's electromagnetic fields.

- ***Emotional Contagion***

Another way to explain empaths is the phenomenon of emotional contagion. This phenomenon is about how most people are able to also experience the emotions of those around them. An example of this can be in a classroom where one young student's crying can make other students cry.

Emotional contagion can easily happen in workplaces and this can either have positive and negative effects. But a good leader can use this to synchronize the minds of the workers positively to have good work ethics and relationships.

Since emotional contagion happens in groups, an empath is most often mindful of the people he surrounds himself. It is important for an empath to be surrounded by good people because he can easily pick up their emotions. Thus, an empath can easily be influenced by them both positively and negatively.

- ***Increased <u>Dopamine</u> Sensitivity***

There are two kinds of empaths—introverted and extroverted. These two types are due to the level of dopamine, a neurotransmitter that sends signals to the mind about pleasures and how to take action to achieve them.

On the one hand, introvert empaths have high sensitivity to dopamine. This makes them need less dopamine. Due to this, they are satisfied by simple things like reading. They also prefer to be by themselves.

On the other hand, extrovert empaths crave dopamine. They need lots of external stimulations to stay happy. They surround themselves with many people and are often found in social gatherings.

- *Mirror-touch Synesthesia*

    In general, synesthesia is a neurological condition in which an individual experiences not one, but two sensations simultaneously in response to a stimulus. For example, you associate words to a certain taste or relate colors to a form of music.

    Conversely, there is mirror-touch synesthesia. It is an ability to sense what other people feel. For example, you witness someone being caressed on the arm. Your arm will also feel like being caressed, too. Mirror-touch synesthesia can explain what empaths experience.

    Empaths feel other people's emotions as if the emotions are their own. Through this, empaths know how to respect other people's thoughts and feelings, even if at times they do not agree with them. Their hearts are open and can tolerate many people due to having a deep understanding of them. But this does not make empaths as sentimental twats. They are highly intuitive people and they know how to discern on things. Many empaths live good and happy lives because of their ability. Empathy, as what Dalai Lama said, is the most precious human quality.

Signs of Being an Empath

- *Sensitive*

    Empaths are known for being sensitive. They are sensitive to everything that is around them, especially to the feelings of other people. Their heightened sensitivity allows them to feel what other people would ignore. Being sensitive is probably the number one sign of being an empath. Take note that this does not only refer to physical sensitivity but also includes things that are not seen especially emotions.

- ***Being Able to Feel the Feelings of Others***

This is a clear sign of being an empath. If you notice that you can feel what other people feel, then you are probably an empath, especially if this kind of event has happened many times in your life. If you are able to sympathize with others and feel how they feel as if you were the one in their place, then chances are that you have an empathic ability.

- ***Strong Intuition***

Since empaths are very open to subtle energy, they usually have a strong intuition. However, instead of seeing, they are able to feel what is going to happen. This is because they are sensitive to the unseen energy around them. By understanding this energy and working with it, they can turn themselves into highly intuitive individuals.

- ***Possesses a Strong Tendency to be Influenced by Others***

Since empaths are very sensitive, it is also easy to influence them. What you think as just nothing may already mean something to an empath. Empaths tend to feel things before others. If an empath is in a group, he might just be the first person who will be influenced

Chapter 1: Empath 101

by the energy of the group. As an empath, you need to be careful with the quality of the energy that you expose yourself to. As a simple rule: stick to positive energy and stay away from negative energy.

- ***People Usually Get to Like You Easily***

  Empaths are easily likable. This is because they tend to understand people more than others. They are able to sympathize with people naturally, and this usually draws people towards them. Using your empathic ability is also a good way to create rapport with people.

- ***Public Places Can Feel Overwhelming***

  Do you find public places to be overwhelming? Then perhaps you are an empath. This can happen especially if you are surrounded by negative people. Most empaths avoid public places because they often have different qualities of energy, which can be very confusing for an empath especially in cases of prolonged exposure.

- ***Having Self-Identity Issues***

    Because of their unique ability, it is common for empaths to confuse their own emotions for those of others. Sometimes this can be really confusing that they will no longer know how they truly feel about something to the point that they do not know who they are. This is why when you are an empath, it is strongly advised that you spend time alone with yourself. This is to allow you to get to know yourself better. By knowing more about who you really are, you will be able to isolate your own identity from the different energies around you.

- ***Need to be Alone***

    Empaths normally feel that they need some alone time. From time to time, they need to be in touch with themselves away from other people. This is because getting too close to other people can be confusing for them. If you are an empath, then you need to devote time for solitude, and you need to do this regularly. Sometimes things can be overwhelming that you need to step back for a while to regain yourself. Do not worry. This is normal when you are an empath.

Chapter 1: Empath 101

You may notice these signs all at the same time or even little by little. Remember that these are your cues that you are probably an empath.

How to be an Empath

Can you be an empath? The truth is that empathy can be learned. If you think that you are not blessed with the ability of empathy, but if you are eager to learn this ability, then do not be discouraged because empathy is something that you can learn and practice:

- ***Be open***

    You open to people, especially to their emotions. Try to feel them as they talk to you. When you attempt to do this, it is important that you give the person to whom you are talking to your full attention. This is a good way to establish a connection with another. Take note that being open is not just an act, you also need to do it

EMPATH

sincerely. Learn to really listen to people when they talk to you and try to feel them.

- ***Meditate***

    Practicing regular meditation is one of the best ways to develop empathy. Later in this book, you will learn notable meditation techniques.

These meditations will not just develop your empathic ability, but they can also help you to control it. Practicing meditation is like giving your whole chakra system a good exercise. It is noteworthy that for meditation to be effective, it has to be done regularly—preferably daily.

- ***Focus shift***

    This is an excellent technique that can help you develop your empathic ability. As its name implies, it is about shifting your focus on yourself to the other person. Learn to be interested in other people, and do not focus on yourself. You should realize that being empathic is not about you, but it has more to do with the person

Chapter 1: Empath 101

with whom you are connecting to. Be interested in others and try to place yourself in their position.

- ***Follow Your Intuition***

Learn to use and follow your intuition.

Unfortunately, many people these days have forgotten to use their intuition that they no longer understand what their intuition tells them. However, do not be discouraged as it is never too late for you to start following your intuition.

But what is intuition? Intuition is the seat of knowledge. It is closely associated with the third eye chakra, which is located right between your eyebrows. Although being an empath has more to do with your heart chakra than your third eye chakra, developing your third eye chakra

13

significantly helps in strengthening your empathic ability.

To develop your intuition, you have to give it a chance to manifest itself. This can easily be done by following what it says. Pay attention to how you feel, or that gut feeling that you have. Remember that the best way to develop your intuition is by using it.

- *Feel*

A simple yet effective way of developing empathy is by using your sense of feeling. Sadly, many people these days ignore their feelings. This explains why so many people are stressed out and depressed. Keep in mind that every time you ignore how you feel, a part of you suffers. If you want to develop your empathic ability, then you should work on being open to how you feel. Listen to it and follow what it tells you. This is the way to better understand its language. Your intuition and your feelings are intertwined. Indeed, this is just like learning a new language. It may be difficult at first, but if you persist, then you will get good at it over time.

- *Read*

Yes, by reading more about empathy, your brain will get tuned to what it means being an empath. Not to mention, this is also a good way for you to learn so much more about empathy. So, after reading this book, feel free to read other books, blog posts, and articles on the subject.

Chapter 1: Empath 101

The more that you read about empathy the more you will understand it and the more your brain will adjust itself to what it means to be an empath. Also, by reading more about empathy, you get to increase your level of interest in the subject.

Are You an Empath?

So, are you an empath? If you are not yet an empath yet wish to become one, then you can start to awaken this ability inside you. Learn to recognize your feeling and use it. Now, if you are already an empath, then you should learn how you can use it properly and effectively; otherwise, it could be more of a problem than a blessing. You need to have a deeper understanding of empathy so that you can live at peace with it. You cannot keep a blind eye on this ability when you have it since it will definitely affect your life significantly. Instead of ignoring it, you should live in harmony with it. To do this, you need to have knowledge and understanding. After which, you should put your newfound knowledge into actual practice.

You should understand as early as now that empathy is a blessing if you know how to use it properly. Therefore, if you are an empath, then consider it as another reason for you to be happy. Now, it is true that there are empaths who consider their gifts as a curse. Normally, this is because of their lack of understanding of their ability. Hence, you are encouraged to read this book carefully and pay attention to every detail. Remember: knowledge is power.

Chapter 2:
Advantages and Disadvantages of Being an Empath

Advantages

✓ *Having an Understanding Nature*

When you have empathy, you will more likely become a very understanding person. This is because you do not just understand people based on what they say to you. More importantly, you will be able to understand how they feel. This is something that most people fail to do. Indeed, although feelings cannot be seen, heard, nor touched, they nonetheless exist, and feelings do not lie. It is difficult, if not impossible, to lie about how you feel. Whenever you feel sad or happy, it naturally reflects itself on the outside. Feelings are always genuine, regardless of whether it is good or bad.

Since you know how other people feel, it becomes easy for you to understand them. This is important especially when it comes to building a good relationship. By being understanding, arguments can be avoided. This is also an effective way to build trust and strengthen a relationship.

EMPATH

Having an understanding nature is good as it is a positive quality. However, never allow people to abuse your kindness.

✓ ***Being Able to Connect to Another Easily***

Since there is this emotional tie that you are able to tap, it becomes easier for you to create a connection. And since you deal with genuine feelings, you can create a meaningful connection. By using your empathic ability, you can make someone feel at ease, even on the first meeting. Needless to say, if you pursue this connection, you can even make it stronger. While most people can only respond to what is told to them, you are able to recognize those feelings which the other person only tries to communicate.

Chapter 2: Advantages and Disadvantages of Being an Empath

By making good use of your empathic ability, people will want to be more connected to you. Since there is a mutual willingness to create a relationship, establishing a connection becomes easy and natural.

Connecting to another human being can be a wonderful experience, especially if he/she is a good person. Remember to use your gift to create meaningful relationships.

✓ ***Sensitive to Subtle Energies***

As an empath, you are expected to be sensitive to the subtle energies around you. It is believed that everything is composed of energy. Since you are able to feel this energy, you can read and understand what it does. You can easily use this to your advantage. However, it should be noted that this is not always a good thing, especially when you have to deal with negative energies. When you deal with energy, the first thing that you should do is to determine if it is positive or negative energy. If it is a positive energy, then you can allow it to affect you. However, if it is a negative energy, then you should always stay away from it.

These subtle energies can have various forms. They can come in the form of anger, peace, happiness, fear, joy, and others. By being aware of the kind of energy that you are dealing with, you will be able to identify the right actions to take.

It is believed that everything has energy. By understanding how subtle energies work, you will also be able to understand the events in the material plane. As you can see, by gaining an understanding of subtle energies, you will also have a better understanding of the material plane. This can be very handy. For example, you will be able to tell if a person is not in the mood or is just about to get mad. You can then take appropriate actions to prevent any unwanted events. It will also teach you to live peacefully and in harmony with everyone.

✓ ***Ability to Take Control of the Situation***

Being an empath will allow you to have a better view of a situation. This is because you know and understand more than what other people do. Having such knowledge will allow you to take control of any situation. By connecting and knowing how people feel, you will be able to determine the best appropriate actions to take. Remember that feelings do not lie. By satisfying how people feel, you can easily gain their trust. Once you have people's trust, it will be easier for you to take advantage and control of a situation. However, do not use your gift as a way to unduly manipulate people. Always have the purest intentions in your mind.

It should be noted that you should never use your empathic ability to abuse people. Instead, always use it to do what is good. Instead of using your ability to take advantage of situations, you should use it to help people, or at least as a way to be more connected with people.

✓ ***Creative***

Empaths are usually very creative. This is because they are strongly connected to their feelings, and feelings have a

Chapter 2: Advantages and Disadvantages of Being an Empath

very powerful creative force. Of course, being creative alone is not enough. You should also use it wisely. Feel free to come up with ways to use your gift in a more constructive manner. After all, there is no limit as to how you can apply your empathic ability. Also, do not limit yourself and be creative in everything that you do.

Creativity can also be accompanied by passion, and this is a powerful combination. Together with a strong will, you can make wonders.

✓ *Ability to "Read" People*

Empaths normally have this natural ability to read people. This means that you are able to understand people on a much deeper level. Since you know how other people feel, you will be more able to understand how they think.

These days, so many people simply want to be understood. However, the problem is that the majority of people pay no attention to feelings. Instead, they only rely on the thinking process of the mind without placing any importance on how they feel. No wonder why they could not understand one another completely.

As you may already know, having understanding is very important in any relationship. Lack of understanding only leads to poor communication, and a poor communication can ruin even a meaningful relationship.

Many times, by simply connecting with a person and knowing how he feels, it would be enough for you to be able to sympathize with him and understand his situation. When a person feels that he is being understood, it produces a positive feeling. Who knows, this can lead to a wonderful relationship. When you feel people, try to understand them with a good and pure heart. You will be surprised just how many people deserve compassion.

It is also important that to be sincere in what you are doing. Understanding people as they are is only possible when you can listen to whatever they have to say. This might need some exercise of patience from time to time. Nonetheless, it is always good to understand people, especially how they feel. This is because even though the modern world tried so hard to make you forget about your feelings, it cannot be denied that so many people are still driven madly by their emotions.

✓ **Deeper Insight**

If you are a real empath, then you will definitely have a deeper insight of things. Not only do you understand people with your mind, but also how they feel. If you come to think about it, this is not just about people. Your ability also applies to people, events, and others. This is because your feelings always have something to say, even though your mind may sometimes not be able to grasp it. When you know more about something and your insight about it expands further, then you will definitely end up with rich knowledge and understanding.

Having a deeper insight does not just allow you to see things more clearly, but it also allows you to take the most appropriate actions in every situation.

Chapter 2: Advantages and Disadvantages of Being an Empath

✓ *Can Experience Life More Deeply*

Life is not just about what you experience, but it is also about how much you experience it. As an empath, you do not just feel what other people feel, but you also get to feel everything more strongly, and so you experience life deeply. Unlike many people who are so used to what they feel that they no longer recognize it anymore even when they feel stressed out, you are aware that there is no such thing as a meaningless emotion. You are open and sensitive to whatever life has to offer. On a more positive note, this also allows you to experience positive energy such as happiness, love, joy, and peace even more. As people say, life is all about experiences. If you can experience things more intimately, then why not?

Disadvantages

× *Being Too Sensitive*

The most common problem of empaths is that they can be overly sensitive. They tend to get hurt or offended easily. Even a slight offense or rudeness might be taken seriously. If you are an empath, then this is something that you should definitely watch out for. Having the ability to experience emotions or feelings on a much deeper level also includes dealing with negative feelings. So, just how should you deal with this? You need to learn to control your empathic ability. A common problem is that people try to develop their ability as much as they could, and yet they fail to realize that doing so also allows them to experience negative things even more. Of course, this does not mean that you should not develop your empathic ability. Rather, you need to learn a simple skill or technique, and that is to be able to identify whether you are confronted with a positive or negative energy. If it is a positive energy, then you can exercise your ability as much as you want and experience it as deeply as you can. However, if you are confronted with a negative energy, then you should learn to step back a bit and control your ability. You should learn and understand human nature. Accept the fact that things are not always the way that you would want them to be. From time to time, you will have to deal with difficult people. You may get hurt or even offended, yet these things are part of life. So do not worry. There is nothing wrong about being sensitive, but you should learn to use it the right way, and you must learn to take control of your sensitivity.

× *Can Easily be Influenced*

Empaths tend to be easily influenced. Although this is something nice if you associate with good and loving people, it can be a problem if you deal with negative people. Unfortunately, in life, you will also have to meet and face difficult people every now and then. If you are not careful enough, then you might absorb their negative energy and become just like them. This is true especially if you are in a group. The consciousness and energy of the whole group can influence you strongly. This is a common problem faced by all empaths. Hence, it is important for you to choose carefully the people whom you mingle with. Keep in mind that nothing can change you unless you allow it to.

Chapter 2: Advantages and Disadvantages of Being an Empath

It is worth noting that energy has two qualities: good and bad. By distinguishing whether you are faced with a good energy or a bad energy, you can decide if you will allow yourself to be influenced. As an empath, you need to learn to take control of things. You can do this by being more aware and observant of what is going on in your life. Therefore, always make sure to spend time with doing some self-reflection. Pay attention to what happens around you especially to the quality of the energy that you are exposed to. Keep in mind that nothing can influence you without your consent.

To make things easier and simpler, just choose to associate with good people. This way, you will not have to worry whether you are being influenced negatively. Good people do good deeds, so you can only expect positive influence. Avoid loud and obnoxious people because they will only drain you of your energy. Negative people are like parasites that will only make you feel bad about yourself. By choosing the quality of energy that you will welcome come into your life, you can take control of the kind of influence that you allow to be a part of your everyday life. Be in control and choose the kind of influence that you want in your life.

× **Energy Drain**

It is common for empaths to feel as if they are drained of all their energy. This normally happens after being exposed to a public place or dealing with a difficult person. As an empath, you tend to have a higher vibration. This makes you a target for energy parasites, also referred to as energy vampires. Many low-life beings will want to cling to you take energy from you. Take note that this does not always mean getting into an argument or a difficult situation. Do you remember a moment when you feel drained after being with someone even if you did not talk to him? You should understand that energy connects and acts even without any physical manifestation. This is another reason why you need to intentionally choose the kind of energy that you welcome into your life. In the following chapter, you will learn about how to shield yourself from energy parasites. As an empath, learning to shield yourself is a must.

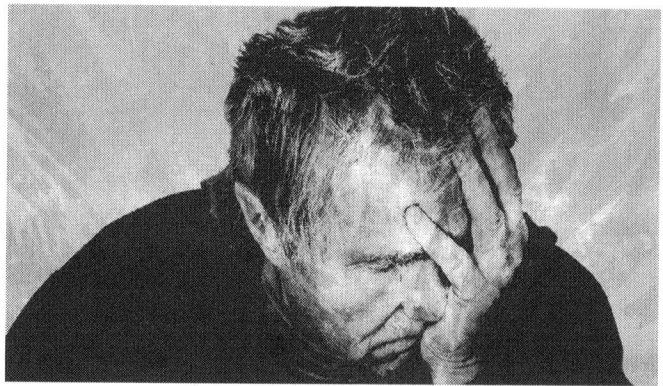

Being drained of energy is not a fun experience. Although empaths can experience this in different ways, the effects are always negative in nature. It can make you feel weak, stressed out, or simply be enveloped in a feeling of sadness. Again, you have to pay attention to the quality of energy that you deal with.

It is also worth noting that is not just people who can drain your energy. There are also places and objects that can drain you of energy. As an empath, you need to

Chapter 2: Advantages and Disadvantages of Being an Empath

learn to use your ability not just to feel things but also for your own protection.

× ***Confusion***

Feeling other people's emotions is not always easy. There are times when it can result in confusion to the point where you do not recognize your own feelings from those of others. This normally happens when you allow certain emotions to penetrate you deeply. In order to avoid this, there are two things that you can do: you should spend more time with yourself to get to know who you are, and you should also learn to exercise non-attachment to things.

By understanding more about yourself, you get to know the emotions that are yours from those that come from an external source. It should be noted that dealing with emotions can be tricky at times, especially if you feel a swirl of different emotions all at the same time. When this happens, just relax and allow the strong current of emotions to settle down. By giving it more time, you can be more in control of the situation and you will be able to recognize your own emotions from others. In case you get confused, wait before making any response. A common mistake is to allow confused emotions to direct your course of action. Never allow emotions, especially the emotions coming from other people, to control you.

The next thing that you want to learn is not to be attached to emotions. In fact, if you give it some thought, even your very own emotions do not always reflect who you really are. This is because many of your emotions are also triggered by other people and events. Let's take sadness, for example. You can be sad not necessarily because you are a sad type of person, but most probably because someone has treated you badly. This is how easy emotions can be triggered by an external force. If you always allow emotions to direct your actions, then you will not be living your life the way you would want to. This gets more complicated when you are an empath, as you will have to deal with different kinds of emotions, including the emotions of other people.

If you ever find yourself confused, you should try to relax as much as you can. You should also not take any action while you are confused. Instead, give it more time and allow the confusion to settle down. Once you are able to clarify the many emotions that you feel, then you can make better decisions and take more appropriate actions.

The key is to not allow yourself to be attached to any emotion or feeling, including your own. This is actually how you learn to take control of emotions instead of the other way around. By recognizing that an emotion or feeling, whether good or not, is not who you truly are, you recognize it to be outside of yourself and so you can control it. In the next chapter, you will realize just how you are not an emotion—not even your own. Instead, you are a consciousness that drifts in infinity.

× *Absorbing Negative Energies*

Just as you can easily connect to energies as an empath, you can also absorb negative energy easily. You should be careful about this as it can be a problem, especially in the long run. Absorbing way too much negative energy can turn you into a negative person.

The thing is that people easily absorb negative energies indirectly. After all, why would anyone want to take in negative energy? You should understand that every time you connect with an energy that has a negative quality, you also get to absorb a part of that energy. The more that you connect and deal with that energy, the more that you absorb it. As you can see, having a connection alone is enough. This is why you need to be careful with the quality of the energies that you connect to.

As an empath, you are like swimming in an ocean of energy. You should realize that you do not have to deal with every energy that you encounter on your journey, especially in the case of a negative energy. Again, you have the power to choose the kind of energy that you welcome into your life.

It is impossible to not absorb any negative energy when you are an empath. However, you can take appropriate actions so that you can choose the exposure that you are willing to handle. Again, avoid loud and offensive people, and stick to those who are good. You should also practice the meditation techniques in this book so that you can cleanse yourself of negative energies. You should know that negative energies attach themselves to those who are in a higher vibration. If you do not take safety protective measures, then negative energies can drain you and pull you down to their level. As an empath, it is your job to manage the negative energies in your life.

You should understand that negative energies are a part of life. However, you have the power to decide how you will react to them. It is also in your power to decide if you will allow negative energies to direct the course of your life. As an empath, it is a bonus that you can sense the feelings and emotions of others. You simply have to use it wisely.

× ***Usually Attracts Negative People***

Empaths usually attract negative people. This is because negative energy likes to cling to positive energy. This is quite an irony in the sense that as an empath, you should avoid negative people. The thing is that many empaths are very kind and gentle. The problem is that they tend to be abused by these negative people.

Chapter 2: Advantages and Disadvantages of Being an Empath

So, what should you do about this? Since you can expect to attract and draw negative people towards you, you should take some preventive measures. A good way to do this is by practicing regular cleansing meditation, as well as avoiding getting too close to negative people.

You should surround yourself with good people. This way you can minimize your exposure to negative people. Also, by surrounding yourself with nice and positive people, you get to draw more positive energy into your life.

When you get to interact with negative people, it is important that you know who you are. This is to prevent being influenced negatively. Indeed, when you are an empath and you spend too much time with a negative person, it is extremely easy to be negatively influenced. This is why you need to know who you are so that you will realize if you are crossing a different line or personality. There are people with empathic abilities who could interact with different kinds of people without any problem; however, this is not easy to do. If you have not yet reached this point, then do not worry. It really takes time and practice to get used to your ability and have complete control over it.

When you have a good understanding of yourself, then you will know if a certain influence comes from an external force. It is then up to you to decide whether you will allow such energy into your life or not. You should also keep in mind that the more negative people that you get to deal with, the stronger you should be.

It is worth noting that interacting with negative people is not always a bad thing. In fact, negative people are said to be the greatest teachers when it comes to developing virtue and wisdom. If you can treat negative people kindly and interact with them effectively, then just imagine how much more you can do it with positive people. Therefore, instead of being scared to be with negative people, you can use them as a means to develop your inner virtues.

× **Can Trigger Fear**

It is not uncommon to find empaths who are afraid of their own ability. This normally happens when you lose control of what you can do and so you start to fear it. When you are an empath, you need to accept that you possess the power of empathy. Take note that this means more than just acknowledging that you possess this ability, but it also means being responsible enough to take positive actions and learn how you can properly and effectively use your ability in your life.

You should not be afraid of who you are. You should not fear your ability. If you, do then that is where it can go out of your control and start to manipulate you instead. The way to combat this fear is to gain the right knowledge. The fact that you are reading this book to learn more about your ability is a good sign. Humans tend to fear those that they do not understand. The problem is that if you feel your empathic ability, then it can easily get out of control and become a problem. So, what should you do? Instead of being conquered by fear, you should embrace what you have. But by

Chapter 2: Advantages and Disadvantages of Being an Empath

accepting your ability, getting to know it, and taking positive actions to live in harmony with it, you can appreciate its value and even be thankful for it. Empathy is a gift, a blessing, as long as you know how to use it.

Chapter 3:
Being Happy as an Empath

Meditation Techniques for Empaths

If you are an empath, then you should learn to meditate. Regular practice of meditation is the way to have control over your ability. The following instructions will teach you important and useful meditation techniques that you can use on a daily basis. But before we discuss the meditation proper, let us first talk about the basics of meditation.

What is meditation?

Meditation is a way to still the mind. There are also people who consider it to be a form of prayer. You can also allow yourself to get in touch with the universal energy and live in harmony with nature.

Whatever meditation is to you depends on the meaning that you give it. The meditation techniques in this book will help you deal with your empathic ability and have mastery over it.

How to meditate?

There are many ways to meditate. The first thing that you should know is the proper posture. There are different meditative postures that you can use. You can meditate while lying in bed, sitting, or even when standing. You can even meditate while walking around. As far as the techniques in this book are concerned, it is suggested that you assume a sitting position when you meditate. Meditating while standing or moving somehow forces you to focus so much on your physical body, while meditating in a lying position can easily make you fall asleep. Meditation in a sitting position allows you to enjoy the benefits of other positions. It is good enough not to make you fall asleep, and it does not draw too much attention to your body. So, how do you meditate in a sitting position? You can do this while sitting on a chair or any flat surface. There is just one thing that you should remember, and this is very important: Make sure to keep your spine straight. This is because the main chakras of your body are located along your spine. By keeping your spine straight, you allow the energy to flow freely within you.

When you start to meditate, you will notice that your mind wanders a lot. You will notice so many thoughts just appear in your mind. In Buddhism, this is referred to as the *monkey mind*. It is the state where the mind is like a stubborn monkey that jumps from one branch to another, so does the jump from one thought to another. Do not worry; this is normal. The more that you meditate, the more you can still your mind. This

Chapter 3: Being Happy as an Empath

is why a regular practice of meditation is important. Meditation is like learning a new skill. The more that you practice it, the better you will get.

Now that you know the basics of meditation, it is time to move on to the meditation proper:

- **_Meditation on the Breath_**

    This meditation is also known as *breathing meditation*. It is probably the simplest kind of meditation. However, do not underestimate the power of this meditation. In fact, there are many meditators who practice this for years. Even the great Buddha used this meditation technique. So, how does meditation on the breath work? The power of this meditation lies in its simplicity. As its name implies, it is about using your breath as the point of focus of your meditation. Before doing the meditation techniques in this book, you may want to create a recorded audio of yourself as you read the instructions so that you can listen to it when you finally decide to meditate. Of course, you are also free to simply memorize the instructions. After all, meditation techniques need not be very detailed and must leave a big room for the exercise of your free and creative mind. Without further ado, the steps are as follows:

    Assume a meditative position.

    Relax.

    Breathe in through your nose, and gently out. Focus on your breathing.

EMPATH

Breathe in, and out. Put all your focus on your breathing and gently ignore all other thoughts that arise in your mind.

You are free to do this meditation as many times as you want and for as long as you want.

Nothing should exist in your mind but your breath.

Regular practice of this meditation will allow you to realize how you are not your body nor your emotions. You are consciousness floating and drifting in infinity.

This meditation also energizes all the chakras in the body. Indeed, although it seems very simple, it is also very powerful that many spiritual masters have used this meditation countless times. Breathe in, and gently out. Focus on nothing but your breath. Be one with your breath. You are breath.

When you want to end the meditation and go back to ordinary consciousness, you simply have to gently think of your physical body and desire yourself to go back to your body. Move your fingers and toes, and slowly open your eyes.

- **Bubble Meditation**

    This is an excellent meditation technique for protection. When you are an empath, you need to protect yourself from negative energies. A good way to do this is by using a psychic shield. This meditation will show you how to create a bubble around you that will deflect negative energies that are directed to you, as well as a

Chapter 3: Being Happy as an Empath

form of protection against the negative energies around you. The steps are as follows:

Assume a meditative position and relax.

Now, imagine you are in a bubble.

This bubble is made of radiant positive energy and protects you from all negative energies.

Visualize the bubble as something very strong and magical.

If you want, you can give it a color, preferably white.

Make it as radiant as you can.

Using your emphatic ability, feel that you have formed a very powerful bubble shield. It is a powerful and most potent protection against all negativity.

Feel free to indulge in this visualization exercise for as long as you want.

Silently affirm: **"This bubble protects me from all negative energies, and it shall continue to do so for 24 hours."**

This means that your psychic protection will only last for 24 hours. You can set a different time, but it is suggested that you do not exceed 24 hours since your shield will tend to weaken over time. If you need more protection when the time expires, simply create another bubble shield.

The key to this meditation is to visualize your shield as clearly as you can. Do not just visualize a bubble by seeing it in your mind's eye but try to make it as powerful as you can. See and believe that you are indeed creating a shield of protection.

In the world of psychism, it is believed that such bubble shield truly exists if you honestly believe that it does. After creating your bubble shield, you can now gently bring your consciousness back to your body in a way that we have already discussed, and you can now face the day assured that you have a powerful bubble shield of protection against negative energies.

Take note that this does not mean that you will no longer be affected by any negative energy, but the shield can at least minimize the effects of negative energies. It might take some practice before you can create a really powerful bubble shield. Just like with other meditation techniques in this book, the key is to practice it regularly. As the saying goes: "Practice makes perfect." The same is true when it comes to learning meditation.

- **White Light Meditation**

This meditation is an excellent meditation to use when you feel drained or simply want to feel better. It is an effective way to charge yourself with positive energy. If you think that you have exposed yourself too much to negative people, then this meditation can help give you a boost. The steps are as follows:

Chapter 3: Being Happy as an Empath

Assume a meditative position and relax.

Now, imagine a powerful ray of divine light descending from heaven and entering the top of your head. This is the white light of pure positive energy.

Visualize and feel how it fills your head with pure energy.

Now, let it descend down to your throat and into your chest. Allow it to fill you completely. From your chest, let it flow down your arms and to your hands.

Next, let it descend further down to your abdomen, down your legs, and down to your feet.

See and feel your whole body as it is filled with this divine light of pure positive energy. As you do, imagine happy events unfold in your life.

Re-experience the happy events over and over again in your mind. Keep your thoughts positive and sound as you continuously fill yourself with the divine light of positive energy.

When you are already satisfied with your meditation, simply visualize the ray of light gently move back up to your head and out back to the heavens.

You should continue to see yourself shining brightly and full of positive energy. See and feel yourself happy and revitalized. When you are ready to end the meditation, simply think of your physical body and will yourself to go back.

Slowly move your fingers and toes, and then gently open your eyes with a smile.

This is a powerful meditation that you can do as many times as you want, especially right after you are exposed to negative energy.

Now, it should be noted that there are those who have tried this technique but fail to experience the enormous power that it offers. You should understand that this meditation lies in your power to visualize. With this meditation, you fill your whole body with divine positive energy. Do not doubt the power of this meditation.

During the meditation itself, you should put all your focus on the steps. That is not the time for you to ask if you are doing it right or not. Also, do not ask yourself the usual doubt: "Is this real?" The time to ask questions and consider your doubts is after the meditation proper itself and not during. Doubts can significantly decrease the effectiveness of a meditation.

Also, asking too many questions while engaged in meditation will only make you divided. When you meditate, you should be as focused as possible. Do not allow your energy to scatter to so many places. Keep all your focus on whatever it is that you need to focus on.

Last but not least, just like other meditation techniques, you also need to practice this meditation regularly. The more that you practice this meditation the more effective it will be.

Chapter 3: Being Happy as an Empath

- ***Cleansing Meditation***

This meditation is similar to the white light meditation, but the main of focus of this meditation is on cleansing you of all negativity instead of charging you with energy. This is an excellent meditation technique to use whenever you feel like you have absorbed lots of negative energy or if you simply want to be more focused and calm. As an empath, it is essential that you learn and practice cleansing meditation regularly. Now, it should be noted that there are many ways to do a cleansing meditation. The method below is one of the simplest yet also a highly effective cleansing technique. The steps are as follows:

Assume a meditative position and relax.

Breathe in gently and breathe out.

As you breathe in, think of happy memories.

As you breathe out, visualize exhaling all stress and problems out of your life.

Now, imagine a ray of light coming from the sky and entering the top of your head. This ray of divine light is a powerful energy of cleansing. Anything that it touches gets instantly cleansed.

Feel and visualize the negative energies in your body as something black. The ray of white light will descend from heaven and cleanse away all negativity.

> *Now, direct this white light to fill the top of your head. As it does, feel and visualize all negative energy that it touches being wiped away. Feel your whole head cleansed of all negativity. Think of happy, relaxing, and positive thoughts.*
>
> *Now, allow this light to fill your whole body. As you do, visualize and feel how it cleanses every negative energy that it touches. By the time it fills your whole body, you will be completely cleansed.*
>
> *Do not rush this meditation. Take as much time as you need. The important thing is to completely cleanse every area where the ray of light passes.*
>
> *When done, simply visualize the ray of light being pulled back up to the sky.*

Although this may seem like a simple technique, it can be very helpful, especially when you feel that you are swamped with lots of negativity. Realize that no matter how much negative energies try to attach themselves to you, they are never a part of you. They cannot harm you unless you allow them to. The more that you practice this meditation the more effectively you can use this technique.

- ***Blessing Meditation***

    This meditation is a way to bless people as well as the earth itself. The best way to deal with negativity is simply by focusing on the positive. For some reason, when you fill your mind with positive things, the

Chapter 3: Being Happy as an Empath

negative energy just seems to dissipate on its own. Here is how this meditation works:

Assume a meditative position and relax.

Place your right hand on your heart chakra. Your heart chakra is located in the middle of your chest. It is the center of your emotions and feelings, and it is the source of universal love.

Now, imagine the person whom you want to bless with the energy of loving-kindness standing in front of you. Feel your love or care for this person.

Raise your left hand in the position of blessing.

Visualize a ray of white light coming from your left hand, and project it to the visualized image of the person in front of you.

Say the name of the person, and then add: **"I bless you with love and kindness. Be happy."**

Once you are satisfied with the blessing that you have given, you are free to visualize another person.

Feel free to bless as many people as you want. Just be sure to do it in a spirit of love and with the purest intention to bless with love and kindness.

Feel free to make some adjustments or changes to the meditation techniques in this book and see what works for you. Remember that when you do these meditation techniques, your intention matters. Consider these techniques as the ways to help you live peacefully with your ability. At the same time, you will be able to enjoy all the benefits of being an empath with fewer issues to worry about.

How to Deal with the Monkey Mind

As already mentioned, the monkey mind is the state of the mind where it jumps from one thought to another without end. This is very common in meditation. In fact, it would be strange if you do not experience it. So, how do you deal with this monkey mind? Is it ever going to stop?

The best way to deal with the monkey mind is simply by ignoring it. If you pay any attention to it, then it just adds another unnecessary thought in your mind. So, instead of being bothered by it, you should focus on your meditation, and be sure that you practice regularly.

When you read books on meditation, you will often read that you should subdue or overcome the mind. However, it should be noted that you do not overcome your mind using force. This monkey mind will not stop no matter how hard you try. A better course of action would be to work in harmony with your mind. Do not build a wall against your thoughts. Instead, allow the thoughts too flow and pass by but do not cling to any of them. Put all your focus on your meditation. After some time of regular practice, the monkey mind will get tired and stop, and you will be in a much better and deeper meditative state.

Chapter 3: Being Happy as an Empath

Important Realizations

- *You are in Control of Your Life*

    Once you learn to live in harmony with your ability, you will realize that you are still in control of your life. Many other empaths who have no knowledge of their ability and do not train themselves end up thinking that their ability is a curse that controls them. Of course, once you know better, you can tell that you are the one in control of your ability and not the other way around. In fact, you are not just in control of your emphatic ability, but you are also in control of your life.

    You should not see your ability as a hindrance to living life. In fact, it will allow you to live a more meaningful life. But of course, before you can take control of your life, you first need to take control of your ability. By now, you already have the keys to take control and mastery of your ability. It is up to you to take positive actions and put your knowledge into practice. Taking control of your ability and your life means so much more than just knowing what to do, but you also need to take actions. If you feel like your ability is the one directing your actions, then that is just a sign that you should do better at controlling it.

    It is also worth noting that the techniques only help to a certain extent. It is also important that you make your own realizations, such as fully realizing that you are indeed in control of your life. Reading books on the subject can only help to show you the way, but you must still take the actions yourself.

Having the right mindset is important. If you convince yourself that you will always have to submit to your ability instead of the other way around, then that is how it is going to be. But, as you already know, things do not have to be that way. With the right techniques and realizations, you can have mastery over your ability and take full control of your life. When this happens, you will realize that the thing that you have been fearing all along is actually a blessing.

- **Stick to Positive People**

You do not have to make things too hard for you. Avoid negative people and stick to those who make you a better person. The truth is that even if you did not have any empathic ability, life would be difficult if you surround yourself with negative people. But, if you create a circle of positive people, life would be so much easier. It is also easier to exercise your emphatic ability if you use it on people whom you really care about. Just be careful not to allow yourself to get too caught up with their problems. If you have to face their sadness, remember that you are not subject to any emotion. You have your very own identity and consciousness. This is something that you will realize especially when you engage in breathing meditation.

Chapter 3: Being Happy as an Empath

Empaths normally draw all kinds of people to them, because they are simply fun to be with. Everyone wants to meet someone who can understand how they feel. This is why so many people like spending their time with an empath. But, as you already know, you do not need to associate with everyone. After all, your ability does not include the responsibility of pleasing every person you meet.

If you come to think about it, sticking to positive people is an advice that is good to follow even if you are not an empath. This is because the people whom you mingle with on a regular basis have a strong impact on your life. By surrounding yourself with positive people, you become more open to positive energies. However, if you fill your life with negative people, then you should also expect to experience negative things. Just as positive people do good deeds, negative people also only do bad things. Since you have the choice with whom to associate with and welcome into your life, it is only right to better stick to good and loving people.

- ***The Importance of Positive Thinking***

    Positive thinking is very important especially if you are an empath. Positive thinking is about filling your mind with thoughts and ideas. As the saying goes: "The happiness of your life depends upon the quality of your thoughts." If you want to be happy, then you should fill your mind with positive thoughts.

    Now, it should be noted that positive thinking is not about denying or not recognizing the negative things in your life. Rather, it is more about facing difficulties and challenges in a positive spirit. Sometimes all it takes is just a switch in perspective. Is the cup half full or half empty?

    Take note that it is not just thinking that matters but also the quality of your thoughts. It is also a good practice to keep your mind positive even when you encounter a difficult situation. You should understand that negative things cannot harm you unless you allow

Chapter 3: Being Happy as an Empath

them to penetrate your mind. Now, although positive thinking is already a common advice, the unfortunate truth is that only a few people are able to apply it properly in real life. A common problem is that many people who want to think positively end up being bothered by negative things. Take note that there is a difference between telling your mind to think positively and actually doing it. Indeed, learning to think positively also takes practice, especially if you are used to having negative thoughts.

- ***Write a Personal Journal/Diary***

    Although not considered a requirement, many advise that you should write a personal journal or diary. This is an excellent way to track your progress. Now, you do not need to be a professional writer just to write a personal journal or diary.

    There are only two things that you should take note of: First, you should regularly update your journal; and second, you should be completely honest with everything that you write in your journal.

    Your journal will allow you to view yourself from a different perspective, from a standpoint that is free from bias and prejudice. In the first few weeks, you might not appreciate having a journal. Do not be discouraged.

    After some time, especially when you start to see your progress, you will begin to appreciate your journal. Keep in mind that your journal should serve as a mirror of yourself. This is why you have to be very honest with everything that you write in your journal and why you should update it regularly.

If you are not fond of writing, you can just write your journal on your computer or even on your mobile device using a writing application. Just be sure that it is secure enough to keep your file. If you are really serious about working on your empathic ability, then writing a journal is strongly recommended.

- ***Group Meditation***

    You might also want to try meditating in a group. Although this is not required, there are many people who find it very helpful. This is because being immersed in such group consciousness can make the experience and power of meditation even more effective. By making a simple search online, you can easily find groups or organizations that might also be into empathy. This is also a good way to connect with

Chapter 3: Being Happy as an Empath

like-minded people. However, it is also true that there are some people who are more effective practicing in solitary or in isolation. Hence, this is a matter of personal preference. Of course, the only way for you to find out if group meditation is for you is me giving it a try. Just to note: All the meditation techniques in this book can be done alone or with others.

- ***Empathy is a Gift***

    Being an empath is a gift. You just have to learn to understand your ability and use it effectively. In fact, these days, there are many people who want to turn themselves into an empath. However, normally, before you appreciate it as a gift, you first need to face some challenges to put it under your control.

    Empathy is a gift not just because it will allow you to "read" other people, but also because you can use it to help others. After all, what good is a gift if you do not use it to help people? Being an empath will allow you to connect with people on a deeper level and be able to understand their position. It is not always that simple to be an empath. As the saying goes, "With great power comes great responsibility."

    Just imagine what you can do and the people you can help if you are able to master this ability. This gift is not just about sensing emotions and energies around you, but it will also enable you to come up with the right actions and turn any situation to your advantage.

EMPATH

If you still find it hard to realize how your ability can be considered a blessing or a gift, it only means that you have not yet taken control of it. Simply stick to the practices in this book and you will soon attain mastery of your empathic ability.

- ***Handle Negative Energies Properly***

You should realize that every negative energy has one good quality: It can be changed. This means that you can turn it into something positive. Empaths are not afraid of negative energies. However, true empaths simply realize that it is better to prefer positive energies over negative. But, you should know that dealing with negative energies is a part of life. Just as every yin has a yang, every yang also has a yin. No matter what you do, you cannot escape from negative energies. Always consider the fact that the world is full of different kinds of people.

The best way to handle negative energy is to not fight it. Simply shift its quality from negative into positive. For example, if you are faced with the negative energy of hatred, then cultivate love and kindness. This is a how you transmit energy from one form to another. As you can see you are manipulating the same energy. You are merely changing the degree or quality.

By focusing on the positive, the negative energy simply "disappears" on its own. The thing is that no matter what you do with a negative energy it is still a negative energy even if you keep it for so long. It is also in the nature of energy to be eternal. You cannot kill energy; it can only be changed from state to state, degree to degree, quality to quality — and yet remains the same energy.

Do not spend too much time thinking about negative energy because it only makes it stronger. After recognizing a negative energy, you should think of the opposite and start cultivating its positive quality. This is how you handle negative energies: you turn them into good.

- ***Be Happy***

Empathy is a gift. Once you know how to deal with it and use it properly, you will realize that it is something that you should be happy about. This is true especially once you learn how to use your ability not only for yourself but also to help people. Be happy. Happiness is also a positive energy that attracts more positive energy into your life. If you are not happy, then life starts to be filled with negative energies. As an empath, you need to be able to sense this in the first instance.

Always strive for happiness. After all, what good is a gift if you are not happy with your life? It should be noted that being happy means so much more than having the desire or simply telling yourself to be happy. What is important is that you take positive actions to be happy. Also, when you are happy, it becomes much easier to use and appreciate your empathic ability. There is also a belief that when a person is happy, his chakras also become much more powerful, and this means having a stronger emphatic ability.

EMPATH

No matter where you are in your journey as an empath, keep in mind that you deserve to be happy. In fact, when you deal with your ability, you should also consider the things that will make you happy. Ask yourself: How can I use my empathic ability to become happier? Visualize having attained such level where you are in control of your ability. Did you realize how much it can help you in your life? It simply makes life more meaningful. Now, I want you to know that whatever it is that you visualize is something within your reach, and you can turn it into a reality. Remember: happiness is a choice. Embrace your empathic ability and live a happier life.

Conclusion

Thanks for making it to the end of this book. I hope it was informative and provided you with all of the tools you need to achieve your goals whatever they may be.

The next step is to apply everything that you have learned and start being in control of your empathic ability and live a happier life. Indeed, being an empath can be quite challenging at first. But, with the right knowledge and perseverance in practice, you can learn to appreciate why it is considered a gift and how you can use it for good. Unfortunately, many empaths are controlled by their ability instead of the other way around. By now, you are already equipped with a strong foundation on what you should do with your ability. This book has given you the keys and it is up to you to apply them and create positive changes in your life.

Finally, if you found this book useful in any way, a review on Amazon is always appreciated!

Made in the USA
San Bernardino, CA
25 July 2018